DUINO ELEGIES

Rainer Maria Rilke

In Translations by M. D. Herter Norton
Letters to a Young Poet
Sonnets to Orpheus
Wartime Letters of Rainer Maria Rilke
Translations from the Poetry of Rainer Maria Rilke
The Lay of the Love and Death of Cornet Christopher Rilke
The Notebooks of Malte Laurids Brigge
Stories of God

Translated by Stephen Spender and J. B. Leishman
Duino Elegies (Bilingual Edition)

Translated by Jane Bannard Greene and M. D. Herter Norton
Letters of Rainer Maria Rilke
Volume One, 1892-1910
Volume Two, 1910-1926

John J. L. Mood
Rilke on Love and Other Difficulties:
Translations and Considerations of Rainer Maria Rilke

Rainer Maria Rilke

DUINO ELEGIES

*A New Translation, with an
Introduction and Commentary, by*

David Young

W · W · NORTON & COMPANY
New York · London

This translation was originally published in FIELD, *Contemporary Poetry and Poetics*, issues 5 through 9.

W. W. Norton & Company, Inc., 500 Fifth Avenue, New York, N.Y. 10110
W. W. Norton & Company Ltd., 37 Great Russell Street, London WC1Ḇ 3NU

Library of Congress Cataloging in Publication Data
Rilke, Rainer Maria, 1875–1926.
    Duino elegies.

    Translation of Duineser Elegien.
    I. Young, David P.   II. Title.
PT2635.I65D82   1978   831'.9'12   78–2816

ISBN 0-393-04501-3

6 7 8 9 0

Contents

Introduction

We have a marvelous, almost legendary, image of the circum-
stances in which the composition of this great poem began. Rilke
was staying at a castle (Duino) on the sea near Trieste. One
morning he walked out on the battlements and climbed down to
where the rocks dropped sharply to the sea. If such a scene makes
us think of Hamlet, about to encounter a ghost or begin a soliloquy,
what follows may remind us even more of Lear, whose mind was
brought to an extraordinary clarity at the brink of derangement,
posing questions about human existence ("Is man no more than
this? Consider him well.") while exposed to the elements. From
out of the wind, which was blowing with great force, Rilke seemed
to hear a voice: *Wer, wenn ich schriee, hörte mich denn aus der Engel
Ordnungen?* (If I cried out, who would hear me up there, among the
angelic orders?). He wrote these words, the opening of the first
Duino Elegy, in his notebook, then went inside to continue what
was to be his major work and one of the literary masterpieces of this
century.

The story has much to tell us about poetic composition: a
heightened awareness in which a voice that is and is not the poet's
begins to speak, almost as if a dramatic character were reciting a
"part," speaking both for himself and for all of us, as Hamlet and
Lear seem to. No wonder the voice of the *Elegies* varies its pronouns
so often, sometimes speaking for Rilke, sometimes to him, and,
more often than not, speaking with mysterious force and urgency
for and to each of us, we who are human, intrigued yet bewildered
by our existence. We cannot read this great poem until we realize
that it speaks in a voice at once deeply personal and piercingly

impersonal: Rilke's voice, Lear's voice, the voice of the wind, my voice, your voice too. To have taken the individual self, communing with itself in profound and frightening isolation, and to have made its solitary voice the every-voice that seems to respond from within us as we read the poem, was a remarkable achievement. In a sense, it reflects the aim of every lyric poem, but the peculiar tension between one self, isolated, and all selves, made one by isolation, that vibrates in the voice of this poem makes it especially dramatic. And even so, Rilke's achievement in the *Elegies* is still not fully grasped. Like the cathedrals that intrigued him, this poem has stood completed in our midst for some time now, but its clarity of outline and abundance of detail, its intimacy and majesty, are still coming into focus.

For Rilke, after that moment in the wind, it was not simply a matter of writing it down. The poem he began that day in 1912 he was to work on for ten years, an act of great artistic patience and restraint. And if the completion was troublesome, coming near the end of Rilke's life, we must also consider the effort that led up to that first outburst. Rilke had not mastered his life or his art with anything like ease. Born in Prague in 1875, he found his poetic vocation after a difficult childhood and then devoted himself to it with a dedication that cut him off from other people. Despite marriage and many friendships, he was essentially solitary, needing isolation in order to journey deeply into himself, where terror, exhilaration, and further solitude lay in wait. He forged his style slowly and with difficulty, out of nineteenth-century Romanticism and the more contemporary movements of Expressionism and Symbolism. He pressed language and imagination for a precision and an intensity that other poets still marvel at.

It was a career marked by restless travel, study, and continued uncertainty about his writing. By the time Rilke had written the *New Poems* (1907, 1908) and, more especially, *The Notebooks of Malte Laurids Brigge* (1910), an experimental prose work that resolutely explored the worst fears that memory, imagination, and existence can produce, he began to think he was artistically blocked and used up. But after two frustrating years, he found he could say, at Duino, "Solitude is a true elixir." Something was beginning to happen. He spoke of himself in letters as creeping around in the thickets of his life, "shouting like mad and clapping my hands...I howl at the moon with all my heart and put the blame on the dogs" (Lear again). But he was also poised and listening, and when the voice came on the wind he was ready: *Stimmen, Stimmen. Höre, mein Herz* ...(Voices, voices. Listen, my heart...). Ten years in all it would last, that listening. A work that would combine the intensity of the lyric with the scope of the long poem, that would allow the poet to stand on the borders of life and death and sing both in anguish and jubilation, was underway at last.

*   *   *

A student once asked me what the *Duino Elegies* were about, and before I had time to begin explaining how impossible the question was, I had already replied: "They are about what it really means to be human." I still like my thoughtless answer. The poem (or poems; it is both one and ten) resists paraphrase or identification, but that it addresses itself to what we call the human condition, with considerable force and honesty, there can be no doubt. It speaks to the distinctive and often crippling effects of our self-awareness, to the alienation from others and from ourselves that we suffer in varying degrees. It touches on children and parents, on love and lovers, on heroes and heroism, art and artists. Through its concern with this last group it deals with our attempts to use our self-consciousness to some advantage: to transcend, through art and the imagination, our self-deception and our fear.

In the process of defining and facing the terms of our existence, the poem is perhaps most famous for speaking trenchantly and courageously of death, the single overwhelming fact of mortality, the most feared and least faced aspect of our lives. Not death alone, of course, but all the things that go with it. Loss, change, pain, illness, irreparable distress. Night-fears. The ache of incessant consciousness, the cauldron of inherited savagery that steams even in children, the sense of being different from the rest of the creation, the terrifying perfection and indifference of the angel.

But these characterizations of the poem's themes suggest an abstractness that it avoids. The *Elegies* are thronged with acrobats, stories, historical characters, myths, statues, cities, landscapes, animals, carnivals, angels, words, a summer morning, dead children, and a host of astonishing metaphors. And always death, a presence, a mystery, looms up, near or far, to give the poem its fullest resonance and meaning. Rilke wrote to a Swiss friend about "the determination constantly maturing in me to keep life open towards death." To his Polish translator, he elaborated the idea:

> *Affirmation of life AND death appears as one in the 'Elegies.'*
> To admit the one without the other is, as is here learned and celebrated, a limitation that in the end excludes all infinity. Death is the *side of life* that is turned away from us: we must try to achieve the fullest consciousness of our existence, which is at home in the *two unseparated realms*, *inexhaustibly nourished by both*....The true figure of life extends through *both* domains, the blood of the mightiest circulation drives through *both; there is neither a here nor a beyond, but the great unity*.... Transience everywhere plunges into a deep being.

Rilke's insights about the interpenetration of life and death do not account for everything the *Elegies* have to tell us, but they make an excellent starting-place for the new reader, for they mark the distinctive territory of the poem (few poets have written so searchingly about the fact and meaning of human mortality) and lead one forward, as the Lament leads the young man through the hushed land of death in the final section of the poem.

Perhaps the reader has noticed that even in explanations like the one quoted above, Rilke resorts to metaphor: nourishment, the circulation of blood, a plunge into a deep. Let this serve to remind us that the poem does not drive toward philosophical statement or toward articles of faith. Its tendency is motion, not rest, and to try to extract a system of thought from it, as readers have learned, is like nailing water or netting wind. Richard Exner spoke recently of Rilke's achievement:

> ...a new language which in turn expresses the very inseparability of intellect and emotion. After all, emotional experiences are expressed in intellectual correlatives, and the intellect interprets the emotional event!... Rilke *never* said I give you the answers. He said love the questions and perhaps you'll live your way into the answers.

There is a further lesson in metaphor. It is a unique instrument of thought, a tool, a sixth sense (or better, an extra eye, extra ear, etc.), a ladder rising from the foul rag and bone shop of the heart, a philosopher's honeymoon, an angel's mirror. And Rilke is a master of it. In an essay on Dante, the Russian poet Mandelstam provides a valuable insight into the way great poetry moves forward through sequences of metaphorical transformation:

> It is only by convention that the development of an image can be called development. Indeed, imagine to yourself an airplane (forgetting the technical impossibility) which in full flight constructs and launches another machine. In just the same way this second flying machine, completely absorbed in its own flight, still manages to assemble and launch a third. In order to make this suggestive and helpful comparison more precise, I will add that the assembly and launching of these technically unthinkable machines that are sent flying off in the midst of flight do not constitute a secondary or peripheral function of the plane that is in flight; they form a most essential attribute and part of the flight itself, and they contribute no less to its feasibility and safety than the proper functioning

of the steering gear or the uninterrupted working of
the engine.

That this description applies to Rilke's method and helps to ac-
count for the exhilaration and difficulty of his poem should be clear
to the reader before he or she is very far into the poem. It occurs
from phrase to phrase, as in the list which constitutes the answer to
Rilke's question of the angels ("Who are you?") early in the Second
Elegy. It develops from line to line and stanza to stanza, as in the
Fourth Elegy, where we careen through natural images—trees,
migratory birds, lions—to the interior landscapes of lovers, to an
elaborate trope based on drawing technique, to waiting in a theater
for a performance to begin, a dancer, a puppet show, then to the
poet's relation with his father (with figures of tasting and spatial
distance) and back to the puppet show, now operated by an angel.
Perhaps most wonderful of all, this transforming process operates
from Elegy to Elegy, as the poem gathers strength and momentum
by recycling and renewing itself. One can read any Elegy by itself,
and one can browse, but to read straight through, from First to
Tenth, is to experience the full cumulative power of the transfor-
mation, the whole flight.

What of the man who made these soaring, changing figures? He
is something of a mystery. He has been worshipped and he has
been reviled. He is accused of narcissism, of inability to sustain full
relationships, of overweening egotism—these 'failings' have been
much discussed. But Rilke was no monster. He gave of himself to
others as he could, when he could, while remaining true in the way
he felt he must to his great preoccupations. Stefan Zweig, who
knew him in Paris, found himself wondering, as he wrote an
autobiography during the Second World War, whether the world
would ever again see people like Paul Valéry, Emile Verhaeren,
and Francis Jammes, artists who renounced the ephemeral and
dedicated themselves fully to their art:

> Of all these men, perhaps none lived more gently, more
> secretly, more invisibly than Rilke. But it was not will-

ful, nor forced or assumed priestly loneliness such as Stefan George celebrated in Germany; silence seemed to grow around him, wherever he went, wherever he was. Since he avoided every noise, even his own fame—that "sum of all misunderstandings, that collects itself about a name," as he once expressed it—the approaching wave of idle curiosity moistened only his name and never his person. It was difficult to reach Rilke. He had no house, no address where one could find him, no home, no steady lodging, no office. He was always on his way through the world, and no one, not even he himself, knew in advance which direction it would take.

The silence which Zweig says grew around Rilke was necessary to that extraordinary and attentive listening of the heart out of which the *Duino Elegies* began. Rilke's way through the world took him to Duino, where the poem began in 1912, and eventually to Muzot, in Switzerland, where it was completed, in a burst that included the *Sonnets to Orpheus*, in 1922. We should be grateful for that silence, that listening, that way through the world: we are their beneficiaries.

NOTES

The first letter quoted ("Solitude . . . put the blame on the dogs") is to Princess Marie von Thurn und Taxis-Hohenlohe, owner of Duino, who had given him its use, and is dated December 30, 1911.

The phrase about keeping life open to death is from a letter to Nanny von Escher, December 22, 1923. Rilke's Polish translator was Witold von Hulewicz; the letter in question is dated November 13, 1925. The part of it which concerns the *Sonnets* and the *Elegies* is translated and quoted in full in M. D. Herter Norton's translation of the *Sonnets*, (Norton, 1942) pp. 131–136.

Richard Exner's lecture, "Alas, poor Rilke; His Readers, His Reception, the Boldness of Fear, and the Language of Fish," was delivered at a symposium in honor of Rilke's hundredth birthday held at Oberlin December 4–6, 1975. It later appeared, considerably expanded, as "Ach, armer Rilke! Leser und Narziss—Kühnheit der Furcht—Zeitgenossenschaft—Sprache der Fische" in *Rilke heute: Beziehungen und Wirkungen* (2. Band) Frankfurt/Main: Suhrkamp, 1976, pp. 59–94.

The translation of Mandelstam's "Talking About Dante," by Clarence Brown and Robert Hughes, was published in *Delos*, 6. The quotation is from page 81.

Stefan Zweig's autobiography, *The World of Yesterday*, was published in 1943 by Viking Press. The quotation is from page 141.

Translator's Note

A number of translations of Rilke's *Duineser Elegien* already exist in English. None is definitive. Probably no single translation ever will be. What made me undertake the present version was a feeling that existing renderings were unsatisfactory in two ways: from the point of view of clarity, and from that of modernity. It seems to me crucial that the reader of a translation *understand* what is being said; that involves, over and over, an urgent search for the exact meaning of a passage, and, equally vital, its clear expression in the language of the translator. True "accuracy" in translation needs to be distinguished from literal sense on the one hand and loose paraphrase on the other. Literal sense fails the translator when he gives a word that has vivid associations in one language a dictionary translation into an inert, uninteresting word in the other language; the process is not at all accurate given the kind of interest that poetry brings to language. Paraphrase, if it is expressive, can be remarkably impressive when we are not in a position to question accuracy. But it invites the translator to introduce subtle (or unsubtle!) changes that withhold the unique sense of the poetic original.

When I say that a reader must understand a translation, I mean to imply as well that his interest must be aroused and held. In this respect, it seems essential to have the Elegies move with energy and sweep, carrying us forward in the current of their excitement. Too often, I felt, one could keep one's attention focused on the existing translations only with effort; like muddy rivers, they were both sluggish and unclear.

The issue of clarity is in this case intertwined with the question of modernity. Rilke began his great poem in 1912, and did not finish it until ten years later. Thus, while it belongs to a tradition and partakes of the 19th century in which the poet came to greatness, it is most definitely a poem of the modern age, a classic of this century like *The Waste Land, The Heights of Macchu Picchu, The Man With the Blue Guitar* and any of Yeats' volumes from *Responsibilities* on. Other translations seemed to me, in matters of diction, imagery, syntax and movement, too willing to face Rilke toward the past, making him sound in English like Tennyson, or Milton, or the Wordsworth of *The Prelude*. If my version seems excessively contemporary to some, it will be because I have tried to bring the poet's voice, in all its life and urgency, to the surface of the poem, free of the mufflings and wrappings of the traditional long poem in English.

The urge to achieve clarity, and the desire to let Rilke's poem speak in the voice of this century's poetry, both depended heavily, I came to feel, on a successful choice of form. As I began work on the *Elegies* I found that the long lines of the original were difficult to reproduce in English (or, more strictly speaking, American). Read aloud, they sounded fine; the listener could follow in the reader's voice the emphases, hesitations, and variations in speed. On the page, however, the long line did not readily suggest the "living" quality, and was one of the features most likely, I came to feel, to make the poem seem like a museum piece. As I was pondering solutions to this problem, I happened to re-read some of William Carlos Williams' late poetry. I realized with a start that Williams' triadic line, made up of three "variable feet," units equal in length of speaking time, was a possible model. Much of Williams' late work can with justice be called "elegiac," and his triadic line combines the comprehensiveness of the traditional elegiac line with the fragmented and eccentric qualities of modern American speech:

Inseparable from the fire
     its light
           takes precedence over it.

Then follows
>   what we have dreaded—
>   but it can never
overcome what has gone before.
>   In the huge gap
>   between the flash
and the thunderstroke
>   spring has come in
>   or a deep snow fallen.

A long line made up of three shorter, overlapping units makes an extremely flexible instrument of expression. The more I have worked with it, the deeper my respect for it has grown. Readers who are initially put off by having poetry "scored" so precisely on the page will find that familiarity resolves most difficulties, and that reading aloud is, as always, the best test of the poetry's efficacy. For me, moreover, the usefulness of the variable foot and the triadic line is again and again bound up with solutions not only to problems of movement and rhythmic control, but of precise expression as well, getting Rilke's difficult German to make clear and interesting sense in English. Two earlier translators of the Elegies, Edward and Vita Sackville-West, compared Rilke's line to "an immense road, admitting many thoughts and images abreast of one another, and seeming to suggest movement in more directions than one." Their solution—a monotonously regular blank verse— is dismaying, but their characterization of Rilke's line is accurate indeed, and helps, I think, to explain my choice.

One further point about my use of the "variable foot." The Elegies were serialized, as I worked on them, over a two and a half year period in the magazine FIELD. During this time my practice with the variable foot changed markedly. My first versions, I came to feel, were too choppy and fragmented, partly from an attempt to stay too close to the lines of the original. I found myself lengthening the variable foot and making it run more smoothly, and I eventually revised all ten elegies to conform to this practice. Thus, the first published version of the First Elegy was 101 lines; the present one is 82 (the original is 95). I also came to feel that normal punctuation, with the exception of commas, was most appropriate; this practice, in fact, reflects Williams' own. The present version, then, represents a fairly considerable revision of the serialized elegies, not so much in terms of phrasing (although a number of early inaccuracies have been corrected) as in line length and enjambment.

I cannot begin to document all the help and encouragement I received in the course of this project, but I am eager to acknowledge the occasional assistance I received from David Walker, Marjorie Hoover, Richard Kent, and Galway Kinnell (who made me reconsider my early handling of the triadic line), as well as the pervasive aid of John Hobbs, who read each elegy in draft and criticized it as poetry in English; of Stuart Friebert, who was characteristically generous with his time and encouragement in considering both German and English, time and again; and of Richard Exner, who urged me to a high standard of accuracy and brought his scrupulous attention to bear on all ten elegies, once through as they were serialized, and then again as I prepared the revised version, with an exemplary patience in helping me unravel the knottiest and most persistent problems. To these excellent coaches, critics, and clarifiers, I gratefully dedicate this translation.

First Elegy

If I cried out
              who would hear me up there
                          among the angelic orders?
And suppose one suddenly
              took me to his heart
                          I would shrivel
I couldn't survive
              next to his
                          greater existence.
Beauty is only
              the first touch of terror
                          we can still bear
and it awes us so much
              because it so coolly
                          disdains to destroy us.
Every single angel
              is terrible!
                          And since that's the case
I choke back my own
              dark birdcall
                          my sobbing.
Oh who can we turn to
              in this need?
                          Not angels
not people
              and the cunning animals
                          realize at once

that we aren't especially
          at home
                    in the deciphered world
What's left?
          Maybe some tree
                    on a hillside
one that you'd see every day
          and the perverse loyalty
                    of some habit
that pleased us
          and then moved in for good.
                    Oh and the night
the night, when the wind
          full of outer space
                    gnaws at our lifted faces
— she'd wait for anyone
          that much desired
                    mildly disappointing lady
whom the lone heart
          has to encounter
                    with so much effort.
Is it easier for lovers?
          Ah, they only manage
                    by being together
to conceal each other's fate!
          You *still* don't know?
                    Throw armfuls of emptiness
out to the spaces
          that we breathe —
                    maybe the birds
will sense
          the expanded air
                    flying more fervently.

First Elegy

Sure, spring depended on you.
        Many stars lined up
                hoping you'd notice.
A wave rose toward you
        out of the past
                or a violin
offered itself
        as you passed an open window.
                These were instructions,
your mission.
        But could you perform it?
                Weren't you always
distracted
        waiting for something
                as if all this
was announcing
        a lover's arrival?
                (Where could you keep her
as long as those
        huge strange thoughts
                are coming and going
and staying the night?)
        But sing, when you must,
                of great lovers:
their fame
        has a long way to go
                before it is really immortal.
Those you almost envied
        the unrequited
                whom you found
more loving
        than the gratified
                the content —

begin again and again
                the praise you can never
                                fully express.
Think of it:
                the hero survives.
                                Even his ruin
is only another
                excuse to continue
                                a final birth.
But nature, exhausted
                takes lovers
                                back into herself
as if she couldn't accomplish
                that kind of vitality twice.
                                Have you thought
of Gaspara Stampa
                hard enough?
                                dwelt on her
so that a girl
                whose lover has disappeared
                                can feel
from that tremendous
                example of love
                                'Make me like her'?
Shouldn't these ancient
                sufferings of ours
                                finally start to bear fruit?
Isn't it time
                that in love
                                we freed ourselves
from the loved one
                and, trembling,
                                endured

as the arrow endures the string
   collecting itself
      to be more than itself
as it shoots?
   For there is no remaining,
      no place to stay.

Voices, voices.
   Listen, my heart
      as only the saints
have listened
   for a gigantic call
      to lift them
right off the ground
   but they go on kneeling
      impossible beings
taking no notice
   that's how completely
      they listened.
Not that you
   could bear hearing
      God's voice
— oh no.
   But listen
      to that soft
blowing . . .
   that endless report
      that grows out of silence.
It rustles toward you
   from those who died young.
      When you went into churches

in Naples and Rome
            didn't their fates
                        touch you gently?
Or else an inscription
            stirred you deeply
                        like that tablet
in Santa Maria Formosa
            not long ago.
                        What do they want of me?
I must softly erase
            my own slight
                        sense of injustice
for it sometimes
            slows down
                        their spirits' pure movements.

Of course it is odd
            to live no more
                        on the earth
to abandon customs
            you've just begun
                        to get used to
not to give meaning
            to roses
                        and other such
promising things
            in terms of
                        a human future
to be held no more
            by hands that can
                        never relax

for fear they will drop you
        and even to put
                your name to one side
like a broken toy.
        Strange
                to wish wishes no longer.
Strange
        to see things
                that seemed to
belong together
        floating in every
                direction.
It's very hard to be dead
        and you try
                to make up for lost time
till slowly you start
        to get whiffs
                of eternity.
But the living are wrong
        in the sharp
                distinctions they make.
Angels, it seems,
        don't always know
                if they're moving among
the living or the dead.
        The drift of eternity
                drags all the ages of man
through both of those spheres
        and its sound
                rises over them both.

Those who have died young
            finally need us no longer
                        — you can be weaned
from things of this world
            as gently as a child
                        outgrows its mother's breast.
But we who have need
            of those huge mysteries
                        we who can sometimes
draw up from
            wellsprings of sadness
                        rejoicing and progress
how *could* we exist
            without them?
                        Is the old tale pointless
that tells how music began
            in the midst of the mourning
                        for Linos
piercing
            the arid numbness
                        and, in that stunned
space
            where an almost
                        godlike youth
had suddenly stopped existing
            made emptiness vibrate
                        in ways
that thrill us
            comfort us
                        help us now?

Second Elegy

Every angel is terrible.
         And still, alas
                 knowing all that
I serenade you
         you almost deadly
                 birds of the soul.
Where are the days of Tobias
         when one of these
                 brightest of creatures
stood
         at the simple front door
                 disguised a little
for the trip
         and not so frightening
                 (a young man
like the one
         who looked curiously
                 out at him).
If the dangerous archangel
         took one step now
                 down toward us
from behind the stars
         our heartbeats
                 rising like thunder
would kill us.
         Who are you?

Creation's spoiled darlings
            among the first to be perfect
                     a chain of mountains
peaks and ridges
            red in the morning light
                  of all creation
the blossoming godhead's pollen
            joints of pure light
                  corridors
staircases
            thrones
                  pockets of essence
ecstasy shields
            tumultuous storms
                  of delightful feelings
then suddenly
            separate
                mirrors
gathering the beauty
            that streamed away from them
                  back to their own faces again.

For as we feel
            we evaporate
                  oh we
breathe ourselves out
            and away
                  emberglow to emberglow
we give off a fainter smell.
            It's true that someone
                may say to us

Second Elegy

'You're in my blood
   this room
      the spring
is filling with you' . . .
   What good is that?
      he can't keep us
we vanish inside him
   around him.
      And the beautiful
oh who can hold them back?
   It's endless:
      appearance shines
from their faces
   disappearing — like dew
      rising from morning grass
we breathe away
   what is ours
      like steam from a hot dish.
Oh smile where are you going?
   Oh lifted glance
      new, warm
receding wave of the heart
   woe is me?
      it's *all* of us.
Does the outer space
   into which we dissolve
      taste of us at all?
Do the angels absorb
   only what's theirs
      what streamed away from them
or do they sometimes get
   as if by mistake
      a little of our being too?

Are we mixed into
       their features
            as slightly
as that vague look
       in the faces
            of pregnant women?
In their swirling
       return to themselves
            they don't notice it.
(How could they notice it?)

Lovers, if they knew how
       might say strange things
            in the night air.
For it seems
       that all things try
            to conceal us.
See, the trees *are*
       and the houses we live in
            still hold their own,
It's just we
       who pass everything by
            like air being traded
for air.
       And all things agree
            to keep quiet about us
maybe half to shame us
       and half from a hope
            they can't express.

Lovers, you who are
       each other's satisfaction
            I ask you about us.

You hold each other.
            Does that settle it?
                        You see
it sometimes happens
            that my hands
                        grow conscious
of each other
            or that my used face
                        shelters itself
within them.
            That gives me
                        a slight sensation.
But who'd claim from that
            to *exist*?
                        You though
who grow
            by each other's ecstasy
                        until drowning
you beg 'no *more*!'
            you who under
                        each other's hands
become more abundant
            like the grapes
                        of great vintages
fading at times
            but only because
                        the other completely
takes over —
            I ask you about us.
                        I know
that touch
            is a blessing for you
                        because the caress lasts

because what you cover
      so tenderly
            does not disappear
because you can sense
      underneath the touch
            some kind of pure
duration.
      Somehow eternity
            almost seems possible
as you embrace.
      And yet
            when you've got past
the fear in that first
      exchange of glances
            the mooning at the window
and that first walk
      together in the garden
      one time:
lovers, *are* you the same?
      When you lift
            each other to your lips
mouth to mouth
      drink to drink —
            oh how oddly
the drinker seems
      to withdraw
            from the act of drinking.

Weren't you astonished
      by the discretion
            of human gesture

on Attic grave steles?
        Didn't love and parting
                sit so lightly
on shoulders
        that they seemed
                to be made of a substance
different from ours?
        Do you recall
                how the hands rest
without any pressure
        though there is great
                strength in the torsos?
Those figures spoke
        a language of self-mastery:
                we've come to this point
this is us
        touching this way
                the gods
may push us around
        but that is something
                for them to decide.
If only we too
        could discover an orchard
                some pure, contained
human, narrow
        strip of land
                between river and rock.
For our own heart
        outgrows us
                just as it did them
and we can't follow it
        by gazing at pictures
                that soothe it

or at godlike bodies
       that restrain it
             by their very size.

Third Elegy

It's one thing
       to sing the beloved.
              That hidden
guilty river-god
       of the blood
              is something else.
What does her young lover
       whom she can recognize
              at a distance
understand of that
       lord of desire, who often
              out of this lonely young man
(before the girl soothed him
       and often as if
              she didn't exist)
raised his godhead
       dripping with what
              unrecognizable stuff
rousing the night
       to a continuous
              tumult.
Oh Neptune of the blood
       his terrible trident.
              Oh the dark wind
sounding from his chest
       through the spiral conch!
              Listen to the night

scooping and hollowing out . . .
    You stars
        doesn't the lover's
delight in his
    loved one's countenance
        come from you?
Doesn't his secret insight
    into her pure face
        come from the pure constellations?

It wasn't you
    oh no
        and it wasn't his mother
who bent his brows
    to this expectant arch.
        Not from your mouth
girl so aware of him
    not from that contact
        did his lips curve
into this fruitful expression.
    Do you really think
        your soft approach
could shake him that way
    you who walk
        like the wind at dawn?
Oh yes you startled
    his heart
        but more ancient fears
crashed down inside him
    at the shock of your touch.
        Call him . . .

you can't free him
            completely from
                        those dark companions.
Of course he *wants* to escape
            and he does
                        and relieved he gets used to
your heart's seclusion
            and takes hold
                        and begins to be himself.
But did he
            ever really
                        begin himself?
Mother
            you made him little
                        you started him
he was new to you
            and you arched
                        the friendly world
over his new eyes
            and shut out
                        the strange one.
Where, where
            are the years
                        when your slender shape
was simply enough
            to block out
                        waves of approaching chaos?
You hid so much from him this way
            rendering harmless
                        the room that grew
suspicious at night
            and from the full
                        sanctuary of your heart

you mixed something human
          into his nightspace.
                    And you set the night-light
not in the darkness
          but in your nearness
                    your presence
and it shone
          out of friendship.
                    There wasn't a creak
you couldn't explain
          smiling
                    as if you had known
for a long time
          exactly when
                    the floor would assert itself . . .
And he listened
          and he was soothed.
                    That's what your
getting up
          so tenderly
                    achieved: his tall
cloaked fate went back
          behind the wardrobe
                    and his unruly future
(so easily mussed)
          conformed to the folds
                    of the curtain.

And while he lay there
          relieved
                    with your image

dissolving sweetly
        under his drowsy lids
                as he sank towards sleep
he *seemed* protected . . .
        but *within*
                who could divert
or contain
        the floods
                of his origin?
Ah, there *were*
        no precautions in the sleeper
                . . . sleeping
but dreaming, but
        running a fever
                how he let himself go!
He, the new one
        the shy one
                how he was tangled
in the spreading
        roots and tendrils
                of inner event
twisting in primitive patterns
        in choking growths
                in the shapes
of killer animals.
        How he submitted.
                Made love.
Loved his own
        inwardness
                his inner wilderness
the primeval forest
        where his heart stood
                like a green shoot

among huge fallen trees.
Made love.
Let it go, went on
down through his own
roots and out
to the monstrous beginning
where his little birth
had happened so long ago.
Loving it
he waded downward
into more ancient blood
into canyons
where Horror itself
lay gorged from eating
his fathers
and every Terror
knew him
and winked in complicity.

Yes, Atrocity smiled . . .
seldom had you
smiled that tenderly, mother.
Why shouldn't he love it
since it had smiled.
He loved it
before he loved you
because when you carried him
it was already
dissolved
in the water that makes
the embryo float.

You see
we don't love
a single season

like the flowers.
　　　　When we love
　　　　　　a sap
older than time
　　　　rises through our arms.
　　　　　　My dear
it's like this:
　　　　that we love *inside* ourselves
　　　　　　not one person
not some future being
　　　　but seething multitudes
　　　　　　not a particular child
but the fathers
　　　　who lie at rest
　　　　　　in our depths
like ruined mountains
　　　　and the dry riverbeds
　　　　　　of earlier mothers
and the whole
　　　　soundless landscape
　　　　　　under the clouded
or clear sky
　　　　of its destiny
　　　　　　this, my dear
came before you.

And you yourself
　　　　what do you know?
　　　　　　You stirred up
prehistory
　　　　in your lover.
　　　　　　What passions

welled up
    from those long dead beings?
      What women
hated you
    what kind of men
      lost in darkness
did you waken within
    his youthful veins?
      Dead children
strained to touch you . . .
    Oh gently, gently
      do a loving day's work
for his sake
    lead him
      toward the garden
let him have
    more than enough of the night . . .

    Hold him back . . .

Fourth Elegy

O trees of life
        when is your winter?
                We're not in tune
we're not instinctive
        like migrating birds.
                Overtaken
overdue
        we push ourselves suddenly
              into the wind
and arrive surprised
        at an indifferent pond.
              We understand
blooming and withering
        we know them both at once.
            And somewhere lions roam
knowing nothing of weakness
        so long as their
              majesty lasts.

But we
        when we're fully intent
            on one thing
can already feel
        the pull of another.
            Hatred is always close by.

Aren't lovers always
        coming to sheer drop-offs
                inside each other
they who promised themselves
        open spaces, good hunting
                and a homeland?
As when for some
        quick sketch
                a contrasting background
is made with great care
        so we can see the drawing.
                No effort is spared.
We don't know
        the contour of feeling
                we only know what molds it
from without.
        Who hasn't sat tense
                before his own heart's curtain?
It rose.
        There was the scenery
            of departure.
Easy to understand.
        The familiar garden
            swaying slightly.
Then the dancer appeared.
        Not *him*! Enough!
                However lightly he moves
he's just disguised
        and he turns into a burgher
                who enters his house
by way of the kitchen.
        I don't want these
            half-filled masks

a doll, a puppet
        is better. It's full.
                I can endure
the stuffed body
        and the wire
                and the face that's
pure appearance.
        Here. I'm waiting.
                Even if the lights go out
even if they tell me
        "That's all"
                even if emptiness
drifts from the stage
        in gray puffs of air
                even if none
of my silent ancestors
        sits by me any more
                no woman
not even the boy
        with the brown squinting eye.
                I'll stay put anyway.
I can still watch.

Don't you think I'm right?
        You, father
                whose life
tasted so bitter
        after you tasted mine
                the first thick doses
of my necessity
        still tasting
                again and again

as I grew up
        and, intrigued
                by the aftertaste
of such a strange future
        tried out my cloudy gaze
                you, my father
who so often since
        your own death
                have had fears about me
deep in my own hope
        giving up that calm
                that the dead have
surrendering
        whole kingdoms of calm
                for my morsel of fate.
Don't you think I'm right?
        And you
                don't you think so?
you who loved me
        for my little beginning
                of love for you
I always lost track of
        because the distance
                in your face
even as I loved it
        turned into outer space
                where you no longer existed . . .
When I'm in the mood
        to wait
                in front of the puppet stage
no, rather to stare
        so intently that finally
                an angel must come

Fourth Elegy

as an actor
　　　　to make up for my staring
　　　　　　　pulling the stuffed bodies
up to life.
　　　　Angel and puppet:
　　　　　　then at last
there's a play.
　　　　Then what we separate
　　　　　　by our very being
comes together.
　　　　Then the whole
　　　　　　cycle of change
finds its first origin
　　　　in the seasons of our life.
　　　　　　　Above us then
and just beyond
　　　　the angel is playing.
　　　　　　Look, surely the dying
should guess how full
　　　　of pretence everything
　　　　　　we achieve here is.
Nothing is really itself.
　　　　Oh the hours in childhood
　　　　　　when the shapes of things
spoke of more than the past
　　　　and when what lay before us
　　　　　　wasn't the future.
We grew of course
　　　　and we sometimes hurried
　　　　　　to grow up sooner
half for the sake of those
　　　　who had nothing more
　　　　　　than the fact

of being grown up.
           Yet we contented ourselves
                    in our solitary play
with permanent things
           and we stood there
                    in the gap
between world and plaything
           in a place that had been
                    prepared from the start
for some pure event.

Who shows a child
           as he really is?
                    Who sets him among the stars
and puts the measure of distance
           in his hand?
                    Who makes the child's death
out of gray bread
           that gets hard
                    who leaves it there
in his round mouth
           like the core
                    of a lovely apple?
Murderers aren't hard
           to comprehend.
                    But this:
to contain death
           the whole of death
                    even *before* life has begun
to contain it so gently
           and not to be angry —
                    this is indescribable.

Fifth Elegy

dedicated to Frau Hertha von Koenig

But tell me
  who *are* they
    these vagabonds
even more transient
  than we are?
    urged on from childhood
twisted (for whose sake?)
  by some will
    that is never content?
Instead it keeps
  twisting them
    bending them
slings them and
  swings them
    tosses them up
and catches them
  they seem to come down
    from an oiled and
slipperier air
  to land on a carpet
    worn threadbare
from their continual
  leaping and tumbling
    a carpet lost in the cosmos

49

stuck there like a plaster
      as if the suburban sky
            had somehow wounded the earth.
And barely there
      upright, showing faintly
            the huge capital D
that seems to stand
      for existence . . . presence . . .
            the relentless grip
rolls even the strongest men
      round and round
            having fun
like Augustus the Strong
      rolling a tin plate up
            at the dinner table.

Ah, and around this center:
      the rose of watching
            blooming
and dropping its petals.
      Around this pestle
            this pistil
smitten by its own
      blossoming pollen
            re-fertilized to bear
the false fruit of disgust
      that they're never conscious of
            the glossiest veneer
lit by the smirk of disgust.

There's the limp
      wrinkled
            weight-lifter

an old man who now
            just beats the drum
                        shrunk in his
mighty skin
            as if it had once
                        held *two* men
and the other
            already lay
                        in the graveyard
while this one
            survived him
                        living on, deaf
and sometimes
            a bit dazed in his widowed
                        skin.
But the young one, the man
            who might be the son
                        of a neck and a nun
tightly and powerfully filled
            with muscle
                        and artlessness.

Oh you, all of you
            who were given
                        to be the toy
of some pain
            when it was still young
                        during one of its long
convalescences . . .

And you especially
            who fall daily
                        a hundred times

unripe, with the plummet
        that only fruit can know
                from that tree
of jointly constructed motion
        (that goes through
                spring, summer
and autumn
        in a few minutes
                faster than water)
fall with a thump
        on the grave:
                sometimes
in a split-second pause
        a loving look
                toward your
seldom tender mother
        may start to rise up
                in your face:
then it loses itself
        in your body
                whose surface absorbs it
that self-conscious
        hardly attempted look
                and again
the man claps his hands
        for your leap
                and before
any pain can get closer
        to your heart
                that is always
galloping on ahead
        there comes that burning
                in the soles of your feet

anticipating what causes it
        and chasing a few
                quick physical tears
into your eyes.
        And still, blindly
              the smile . . .

O take it, angel!
        pluck it
              this small-flowered
healing herb
        and go get a vase for it
              preserve it!
Put it with those joys
      that *still* aren't
           open to us
praise it
        in a lovely urn
           with a florid
soaring inscription:
        Subrisio
        Saltat.
And then you
      darling, you
           whom the most
delicious pleasures
      have leaped right over
           silently.
Maybe your frills
      are happy for you —
           or the green

metallic silk
        tight across
                your hard young breasts
feels that it's
        endlessly pampered
                and in need of nothing.
You
        set out on display
                again and again
but differently each time
        like the indifferent fruit
                on the wavering
pans of the balance
        in public
                below the shoulders.

Where, oh *where*
        is that place
                — I carry it in my heart —
where for a long time
        they *couldn't* perform
                but fell away from each other
like mating animals
        badly paired
                where the weights
are still heavy
        where the plates
                still wobble off
the fruitlessly
        twirling sticks . . .

And suddenly
            in this difficult Nowhere
                        suddenly the ineffable
place where the pure
            "Too-little"
                        incredibly transforms itself
somersaulting
            into that empty
                        "Too-much."
Where the problem that had
            so many digits
                        comes out right
with nothing left over.

Squares
            oh square in Paris
                        infinite showplace
where the milliner
            Madame Lamort
                        slings and winds
the restless
            ways of the world
                        endless ribbons
finding new loops for them
            frill flowers
                        cockades
artificial fruits
            — all falsely dyed
                        for the cheap winter hats
of Destiny.

.   .   .   .

Angel: suppose there's a place
            we don't know of
                        and there
on an indescribable carpet
            lovers could show
                        the feats they aren't
able to show here
            the daring high figures
                        of the heart's leap
their towers of ecstasy
            their ladders long since
                        propped against each other
where there was never any ground
            trembling
                        and they *could*
before the surrounding
            spectators, the hushed
                        innumerable dead:
wouldn't those dead
            throw them then
                        their forever hoarded
and hidden
            unknown to us
                        but eternally current
coins of happiness
            at the feet of the pair
                        whose smile was finally
truthful there
            on that fulfilled
                        carpet?

Sixth Elegy

Fig tree
        for a long time
                it's meant a lot to me
how you almost completely
        skip blossoming
                and press your purest secret
unglorified
        ahead of time
                into your definite fruit.
Like the pipe
        of a fountain
                your arching boughs
drive the sap down
        drive it up
                and it springs from sleep
hardly awake
        to the joy of its
                sweetest achievement.
See:
        like the god
                into the swan.

                . . . But we
we linger, alas
        our honor lies
                in our blooming

and we're betrayed
            by the time we enter
                        the overdue core
of our ultimate fruit.
            Only for a few
                        the urge to action
rises so strongly
            that they're already
                        standing by
glowing
            in the fullness of their hearts
                        when the temptation to bloom
touches their young mouths
            and eyelids
                        like soothing night air:
heroes, maybe
            and those who are meant
                        to disappear early
whose veins
            Death the gardener
                        has twisted differently.
They hurtle ahead
            in advance of their own smiles
                        like the team
of charging horses
            before the conquering king
                        in the mild, molded reliefs
at Karnak.

The hero is strangely close
            to those who died young.
                        Permanence

doesn't interest him.
        His dawn is his lifetime.
             He constantly
takes himself off
        and enters
             the changed constellation
of his everlasting risk.
        Few could find him there.
             But that dark Fate
who has nothing to say for us
        suddenly all inspired
             sings him on into the storm
of his uproarious world.
        I hear no one like him.
             All at once
his dimmed note
        carried on rivering air
             sounds through me.

Then how I'd like to hide
        from this great longing!
             If I were, oh
if I were a boy
        and still had the chance
             still sat
arms propped on the future
        and read about Samson
             how his mother gave birth
to nothing and then
        to everything.
             Wasn't he hero already
inside you, mother
        and didn't his
             imperious choosing

begin there within you?
          Thousands were brewing
              in the womb
wishing to be *him*
        but look:
            he took hold
he discriminated
          chose and accomplished.
             And if he ever
broke pillars apart
         it was when he burst out
            of the world of your body
into a narrower world
        where he went on
            choosing, accomplishing.
Oh mothers of heroes!
        sources of such
           torrential rivers!
You gorges in which
        virgins have already
           plunged, weeping
from the heart's high rim
        future offerings
           to the son.

For whenever the hero
        stormed through the stations of love
           each heart that beat
for his sake
        only lifted him higher
           and, already turning away
he stood
        at the end of the smiles
           transformed.

Seventh Elegy

No more wooing, voice
      you're outgrowing that
            don't let your cry
be a wooing cry
      even though it could be
            as pure as a bird's
that the season lifts up
      as she herself rises
            nearly forgetting
that it's just
      a fretful creature
            and not some single heart
to be tossed
      toward happiness
            deep into intimate skies.
Like him you want
      to call forth a still
            invisible mate
a silent listener
      in whom a reply
            slowly awakens
warming itself
      by hearing yours
            to become
your own
      bold feeling's
            blazing partner.

Oh and spring
           would understand
                      — not one crevice
that wouldn't echo
           annunciation.
                      The first small
questioning flutenotes
           reinforced by echoing stillness
                      that rises all round
in the pure, affirmative day.
           Then on up the steps —
                      a call that climbs
each air-stair
           toward the dreamed
                      temple of the future
then the trill
           the fountain
                      whose rising jet
catches the falling water
           up again
                      in a game of promising . . .
And all before it
           the Summer.
                      Not only those
summer mornings
           not only the way
                      they change into day
glowing because of the sunrise.
           Not only the days
                      gentle among the flowers
while strong and enormous
           overhead, among the great
                      shapes of the trees.

Seventh Elegy

Not only the devotion
        of these unfolded powers
                not only the roads
not only the evening meadows
        not only the clear breathing
                that follows afternoon thunderstorms
not only approaching sleep
        and a premonition
                late evening . . .
But the nights!
        but the high summer nights
                but the stars
stars of the earth.
        Oh to be dead
                one of these days
and to know that *they*
        are infinite
                all of the stars
for how
        how
                how to forget them!

You see, I've called for a lover.
        But it wasn't just she
                who would come.
Girls would come out of
        inadequate graves
                and stand near . . .
Well how could I
        limit my call
                after I'd called it?

The buried are always
        seeking the earth again.
                You children
one single thing
        fully grasped
            here and now
would be valid
        for many.
              Don't suppose
that fate's any more
        than childhood's density.
              How often you really
overtook your lover
        breathing, breathing deep
            after a marvelous run
toward nothing more
        than the open air.

Just to *be* here
        is a delight!
              You knew that too
you girls who seemed
        deprived of it
            you who were sunk
in the city's worst alleys
        festering there, or exposed
            to its garbage and filth.
For each had an hour
        or maybe not even that much
            just some unmeasurable

moment of time
        between two whiles
                when she had existence
completely
        down to her fingertips!
                It's just that we forget
so easily
        what our genial neighbor
                neither approves of
nor grudges us.
        We want it visible
                to show
when even the most
        visible joy
                will reveal itself
only when we have
        transformed it within.

There's nowhere, my love
        the world can exist
                except within.
Our lives are used up
        in transformations
                and what's outside us
always diminishing
        vanishes.
                Where a solid house
once stood
        a wholly fictitious image
                cuts in, just as if

the whole thing existed
           completely in the brain.
                       The Zeitgeist creates
huge silos of power
           that are as shapeless
                       as the straining urge
he acquires from everything else.
           He has forgotten the temples.
                       We are the ones
who try surreptitiously
           to save such squanderings
                       of the heart.
Yes, where one still stands
           a thing that once was
                       prayed to, knelt to,
served — it reaches
           just as it is
                       into the unseen world.
Many don't notice
           and miss the chance
                       to build it now
inside themselves
           with pillars and statues
                       greater than ever!

Every heavy
           turning back of the earth
                       has such disinherited ones
who possess
           neither earlier things
                       nor what's to come.

For what's ahead
>> is distant for men.
>>>> This shouldn't confuse *us*

it should confirm
>> our preserving a form
>>>> we still recognize:

This *stood* among men
>> at one time
>>>> stood in the midst of fate

of destructive fate
>> stood in the midst of not
>>>> knowing where to go

as if it existed
>> and bent the stars
>>>> down toward it

from the established heavens.
>> Angel!
>>>> I'm showing it to you

there it is!
>> let it stand
>>>> so that you see it

redeemed at last
>> upright.
>>>> Columns, pylons,

the Sphinx
>> the cathedral's gray
>>>> determined thrust

from some fading
>> or unknown city.

>> Wasn't this like a miracle?

Gaze at it, angel
    it's *us*
        you mighty being
you tell them that we could
    accomplish such things
        my breath isn't enough
for such celebration.
    For it seems after all
        that we haven't neglected
the spaces
    our generous portion
        these spaces — *ours*
(How frighteningly vast
    they must be
        if thousands of years
of our feelings
    have not overcrowded them.)
        But a tower was great
wasn't it?
    Oh angel it was
        it was great
even set next to you.
    Chartres was great
        and music reached
even higher
    climbing beyond us.
        Even a girl in love
alone at night
    by her window
        didn't she reach to your knee?

Don't think I'm wooing you!
      Angel
           even if I am
you won't come
      for my call
           is always full of rising
you can't move
      against such a current
           it's just too strong.
My call is an outstretched arm
      and its high, reaching
           open hand
is always before you
      open
           incomprehensible being
wide open
      to defend
           to warn off.

Eighth Elegy

dedicated to Rudolf Kassner

With its whole gaze
         a creature
                looks out at the open.
But our eyes
         are as though turned in
                and they seem to set traps
all around it
         as if to prevent
                its going free.
We can only know
         what *is* out there
                from an animal's features
for we make even infants
         turn and look back
                at the way things are shaped
not toward the open
         that lies so deep
                in an animal's face.
Free from death.
         Because we're the ones
                who see death.
The animal that's free
         always has
                its destruction behind it

and God ahead of it
   and when it moves
      it moves forward
forever and ever
   like a flowing spring.

       We never have
even for one single day
   that pure space before us
      that flowers can open
endlessly into.
   It's always *world*
      it's never a nowhere
where there isn't
   any 'no,' any 'don't'
      never the pure
the untended thing
   you breathe
      and endlessly *know*
and never desire:
   what a child
      sometimes gives himself up to
and grows still
   and has to be
      shaken out of.
Or another one dies
   and then *is* it.
      For when you get close to death
you don't see death anymore
   you look out *past* it
      and maybe then

with an animal's wide gaze.
        Lovers, if they weren't
            blocking each other's view
are close to it
        marveling . . .
           As if by an oversight
it opens up to them
        behind each other . . .
           But neither one can get past
and again
        world comes back to them.
           Always when we face
the creation
        we see only
           a kind of reflection
of the freedom
        that we ourselves have dimmed.
           Or it happens
that an animal
        some mute beast
           raises its head
and imperturbably
        looks right through us.
           That's what fate means:
to be facing each other
        and nothing but each other
           and to be doing it forever.

If the animal
        coming toward us so surely
           from another direction

had our kind of consciousness
          he'd drag us around in his sway.
               But his being
is infinite to him
          incomprehensible, and without
               a sense of his condition
pure as his gaze.
          And where we see the future
               he sees everything
and himself *in* everything
          healed and whole
               forever.

And yet within
          the warm and watchful beast
               there's the weight and care
of a huge sadness.
          For there clings to him
               something that often
overwhelms us
          — memory
               a recollection that
whatever we're striving for now
          was once closer and truer
               and that its union with us
was incredibly tender.
          Here everything is distance
               there it was breath.
After the first home
          the second seems hybrid
               and windy.

Eighth Elegy

Oh the bliss
        of the *little* creature
                that *stays* forever
inside the womb that conceived it.
        Oh happiness of the gnat
                still hopping *within*
even on its wedding day:
        for womb
                is everything.
And look at the
        half assurance of the bird
                that almost seems to know
both states from his origin
        like the soul of an Etruscan
                come from a dead man
stowed in a space
        with his own resting figure
                as the lid.
And how bewildered
        is something that has to fly
                if it came from a womb.
As though terrified of itself
        it shivers through the air
                the way a crack
goes through a cup
        the way a bat's track tears
                through the porcelain of evening.

And we:
        spectators, always
                everywhere

looking at all of that
        never beyond!
                It fills us too full.
We set it right.
        It disintegrates.
                We set it right again
and we disintegrate too.

Who has turned us around this way
        so that we're always
                whatever we do
in the posture of someone
        who is leaving?
                Like a man
on the final hill
        that shows him
                his whole valley
one last time
        who turns and stands there
                lingering —
that's how we live
        always
                saying goodbye.

Ninth Elegy

Why, if it's possible
   to spend our little
      span of existence
as laurel
   slightly darker
      than all the other greens
with tiny waves
   on each leaf's rim
      (like a wind's smile)
— why then
   still insist
      on being human
and shrinking from fate
   long for it too? . . .

   Oh, not because happiness
— that part of approaching ruin
   that rushes ahead of it —
      is *real.*
Not out of curiosity
   not to exercise the heart
      that would have been fine
in the laurel . . .
   But just because to be here
      means so much

and because
        everything here
                all this that's disappearing
seems to need us
        to concern us
                in some strange way
we, who disappear
        even faster!
                It's *one* time
for each thing
        and *only* one.
                Once and no more.
And the same for us:
        once.
                Then never again.
But this once having been
        even though only once
                having been *on earth*
seems as though
        it can't be undone.

And so we push ourselves
        wanting to master it
                wanting to hold it all
in our own two hands
        in the overloaded gaze
                and the dumbstruck heart.
Trying to become it.
        To give it to someone?
                No, we'd like most

to keep it all ourselves
        forever . . .
                Ah, but what
can we take across
        to the other realm
                when we leave?
Not our perception
        learned here so slowly
                and nothing
that's happened here.
        Not one thing.
                So that means we take pain.
Take, above all
        the heaviness of existing
                take the long
experience of love
        take
                truly unsayable things.
But later
        under the stars
                why bother?
They are *better*
        at the unsayable.
                After all, isn't what
the wanderer brings back
        from the mountain slopes
                to the valley
not a handful of earth
        that no one could *say*
                but rather a word
hard-won, pure,
        the yellow and blue
                gentian?

Are we on this earth to say:
              House
                          Bridge
Fountain
              Jug   Gate
                          Fruit-tree   Window
at best:
              Column . . .
                          Tower . . .?
but to *say* these words
              you understand
                          with an intensity
the things themselves
              never dreamed they'd express.
                          Isn't the earth's
hidden strategy
              when she so slyly
                          urges two lovers on
that each and every thing
              should be transformed
                          by the delight
of sharing their feelings?

              Threshold:

what it means
              to two lovers
                          that they too
should be wearing down
              an old doorsill
                          a bit more

after the many
    before them
        and before
the many to come
        . . . lightly.

Here is the time
    for the *sayable*
        here is its home.
Speak, bear witness.
        More than ever
            things fall away from us
livable things
    and what crowds them out
        and replaces them
is an event
    for which there's no image.
        An event
under crusts
    that will tear open
        easily
just as soon
    as it outgrows them
        and its interests
call for new limits.
        Between the hammer strokes
            our hearts survive
like the tongue
    that between the teeth
        and in spite of everything
goes on praising.

Praise the world
        to the angel
                not the unsayable
you can't impress him
        with sumptuous feelings —
                in the universe
where he feels things
        so fully
                you're just a novice.
Show him, then,
        some simple thing
                shaped by its passage
through generations
        that lives as a belonging
                near the hand, in the gaze.
Tell him of Things.
        He'll stand more astonished
                than you did
beside the rope-maker
        in Rome, or the potter
                by the Nile.
Show him how happy
        a thing can be
                how blameless and ours
how even the wail of sorrow
        can settle purely
                into its own form
and serve as a thing
        or die into a thing
                to a realm where even
the violin can't recall it.
        And these things
                that take their life

from impermanence
        they understand
                that you're praising them:
perishing, they trust
        to us — the most
                perishable of all —
for their preservation.
        They want us to change them
                completely
inside our invisible hearts
        into — oh endlessly —
                into ourselves!
Whoever we might
        turn out to be
                at the end.

Earth, isn't this
        what you want:
                rising up
inside us *invisibly*
        once more?
                Isn't it your dream
to be invisible someday?
        Earth! invisible!
                what is it
you urgently ask for
        if not transformation?
                Earth, my love
I will do it.
        Believe me
                your springtimes

are no longer needed
             to win me — *one*
                          just one, is already
too much for my blood.
             I have been yours
                          unable to say so
for a long time now.
             You were right
                          always
and affable Death
             is your own
                          holy notion.

Look, I'm living.
             On what?
                          Neither my childhood
nor my future
             is growing smaller . . .
                          Being
in excess
             wells up
                          in my heart.

Tenth Elegy

That someday
         at the close of this
                  fierce vision
I might sing praise
         and jubilation to
                  assenting angels.
That the heart's
         clear-striking hammers
                  might not falter
from landing on
         slack or doubtful
                  or snapping strings.
That my face, streaming
         might make me
                  more radiant
that this homely weeping
         might bloom.
                  Oh you nights
that I grieved through
         how much you will
                  mean to me then.
Disconsolate sisters
         why didn't I kneel
                  more fully
to accept you
         and lose myself more
                  in your loosened hair?

How we squander our sorrows
        gazing beyond them
                into the sad
wastes of duration
        to see if maybe
                they have a limit.
But they are
        our winter foliage
                our dark evergreens
one of the seasons
        of our secret year
                — and not only a season
they are situation,
        settlement, lair,
                soil, home.

It's true, though:
        how strange are the back streets
                of Pain City
where, in the false silence
        created from too much noise
                there swaggers out
the slop that's cast
        from the mould of emptiness
                the gilded hubbub
the bursting monument.
        Oh how an angel
                would stamp out their
Consolation Market
        leaving no trace
                — the church beside it too

bought ready-made
        as swept and shut tight
              and disappointed
as a post office
        on Sunday.
              Out further, though
there are always
        the rippling edges of the Fair.
              Freedom's swing-rides!
Zeal's divers and jugglers!
        And tarted-up Good Luck's
              lifelike shooting range
where the tin targets
        ring and flop over
              when a better shot hits them.
From cheer to chance
        he lurches on
              since booths
to please all curiosities
        babble and drum
              and tout their wares.
Special Attraction for Adults:
        How Money Reproduces
              Anatomically Valid
Not Just Entertainment
        Money's Own Genitals
              Nothing Left Out
The Act Itself
        It's Educational
              and It Helps
Make You Potent . . .
        Oh, but just outside
              beyond the last

billboard plastered
        with ads for "Deathless"
            that bitter beer
that tastes sweet
        to its drinkers
            as long as they keep chewing
fresh distractions —
        just behind that billboard
            right there
everything's *real.*
        Children play there
            and lovers embrace
off to one side
        so seriously
            in the sparse grass
where dogs do doggy things.
        The young man is drawn
            further — maybe he's fallen
in love with a young Lament . . .
        He follows her into the meadows
            she says:
It's a long way.
        We live out there . . .
        Where?
And the young man follows.
        Roused by the way she moves.
            Her shoulder, her neck —
maybe she comes from
        a splendid race.
            But he leaves her
goes back, turning
        to wave . . . What's the use?
        She's just a Lament.

Tenth Elegy

Only those who've died young
      in their first state
            of timeless calm
— their weaning —
      follow her lovingly.
            She waits for young girls
and befriends them.
      Gently she shows them
           what she wears.
Pearls of pain
      and the fine-spun
           veils of Patience.
With young men
      she walks along
           in silence.

But there where they live
      in the valley
           one of the older Laments
answers the youth
      when he questions her:
           We were once
she says,
      a great race
           we Laments.
Our fathers
      worked the mines up there
           in the mountain-range
sometimes among men
      you'll find a polished
           lump of primeval Pain

or the petrified slag
      of Anger from
            an old volcano.
Yes, that came from up there.
      We used to be rich.

And she leads him lightly
      through the broad
            landscape of Lamentation
shows him the columns of temples
      or the ruins of castles
            from which the Lords of Lament
once ruled the land wisely.
      Shows him the tall tear trees
            and the fields of sadness in bloom
(what the living know only
      as tender foliage)
            shows him the herds of grief
pasturing
      and sometimes
            a bird startles
and writes
      as it flies flatly
            through their field of vision
the image of its
      solitary cry.
            In the evening
she leads him to the graves
      of the ancients
            of the race of Laments
the sibyls
      and the lords of warning.
            But when night comes

they go more slowly
   and soon there looms ahead
     in the moonlight
the sepulcher
   that watches over everything.
     Twin brother
to the one on the Nile
   the tall Sphinx
     the silent chamber's
countenance.
   And they marvel
     at the regal head
that has silently
   and forever
     set the human face
to be weighed
   on the scale
     of the stars.

His sight, still dizzy
   from early death
     can't grasp it.
But hers
   frightens the owl
     from behind the rim
of the crown.
   And the bird
     brushing with slow
downstrokes
   along the cheek
     — the one

with the roundest curve —
           inscribes faintly
                      on the new sense of hearing
that follows death
           an indescribable outline
                      as if on the doubly opened
page of a book.

And higher up, the stars.
           New ones.
                      Stars of the Painlands.
Slowly, the Lament
           tells him their names:
                      "Here — look:
the Rider
           the Staff
                      and that dense constellation
they call the Fruitgarland.
           Then further up
                      toward the Pole:
the Cradle, the Path
           the Burning Book
                      the Puppet, the Window.
But in the southern sky
           pure as within the palm
                      of a consecrated hand
the clear, shining M
           that stands for the Mothers . . . ."

But the dead man
           must go on
                      and silently

the older Lament
        takes him as far as the gorge
             where the spring
the source of Joy
        shimmers in moonlight.
             She names it with reverence
saying:
        "In the world of men
             this is a life-bearing stream."

They stand
        at the foot
             of the mountain
and there
        she embraces him
             crying.

Alone, he goes off climbing
        into the mountains
             of primal Pain.
And not even
        his footstep
             rings from this soundless fate.

Yet if these
        endlessly dead
             awakened a simile for us
look, they might point
        to the catkins
             hanging from empty hazeltrees

or else they might mean the rain
        that falls on the dark earth
            in spring.

And we
        who always think
            of happiness *rising*
would feel the emotion
        that almost startles us
            when a happy thing *falls.*

Notes and Comments

First Elegy

The traditional beginning of a long poem is an invocation, asking for help from a divine source, a muse. Rilke's is the opposite, a turning away, a refusal. The poet is on his own, considering what poetry can be without supernatural sanctions. But if the poet cannot expect contact with angels, he must nevertheless be attentive to the fact and meaning of death. The invocation gradually takes the form of a willingness, even a desire, to listen to what the dead have to tell us. The distinctions between death and life are re-examined. If the dead do not need us, we begin to realize, we do need them. Music, for example, had its origin in the ancient experience of grief.

angelic orders: Rilke's angels, as the poem makes clear, are not those of Christian orthodoxy. He once noted that they were more like those of Islam. The best definition of them remains the poem itself.

Gaspara Stampa: an Italian poet of the 16th Century. Abandoned by her lover, she responded not with despair but by writing poetry and venturing into other love affairs. She died at the age of thirty-one.

Santa Maria Formosa: a church in Venice Rilke had visited in 1911.

Linos: a vegetation god similar to Adonis. It seems likely that Rilke supposed his mourner to be Orpheus, the legendary first poet and musician. It is as though the first experience of grief produced the first music.

Second Elegy

The poem's tendency to use motifs both of image and idea is clear as Rilke again takes up the matter of contact with the angels. This time, though, the focus is not so much the role of the poet as the meaning of our mutability, our ephemeral place in the world. Lovers seem to be in touch with a more lasting existence, a greater reality, but they cannot sustain it. Greek funerary sculpture (*steles* are stone slabs carved in relief) shows, in its dignity and restraint, an acceptance of human transience, and we need an equivalent that we can't seem to find in today's pictures or statuary.

Tobias: in the apocryphal Book of Tobit, the angel Raphael guides Tobias, who does not recognize him, on a difficult journey.

Third Elegy

The exploration of love continues, and a new motif, that of the child, makes its appearance. Again, we seem to have an equivalent to a traditional feature of the epic: the descent to the underworld. Here the journey is interior, reflecting Rilke's interest in the contemporary development of Freudian psychology. In its treatment of the child, the mother, the young man and the girl who is in love with him, this Elegy is an extraordinary mixture of bitterness and tenderness.

Fourth Elegy

Again, lovers, interior landscape, child and parent, this time the father. And new images—theatrical entertainment, with the puppet preferred to the dancer. The boy with the squint is Rilke's cousin Egon, who died young and is commemorated in the *Sonnets to Orpheus*, II, 8. The German word for puppet, *puppe*, also means doll, making the transition to the child among his playthings even more natural. The image of the child will remind some readers of Wordsworth, but Wordsworth's has intimations of immortality, while Rilke's is closer to an understanding and acceptance of death.

Fifth Elegy

In the summer of 1915 Rilke stayed in Frau Hertha von Koenig's Munich apartment, where Picasso's painting of a performing troup, *Les Saltimbanques*, hung (it is now in the National Gallery in Washington). This Elegy is partly inspired by that painting. Rilke seems to have noticed that the group of clowns forms a D shape, and he takes that to stand for *Dastehn*, "thereness," or "standing-thereness," with overtones of *Dasein*, "existence." The problem of making the D the capital letter of a word in English ("Duration"?) is the sort of thing that makes translators despair.

Augustus the Strong: Elector of Saxony, 1670–1733, who practiced feats of strength to entertain his guests, here bending a pewter plate with one hand.

the rose of watching . . . : a good example of Rilke's imagery at its most complex. The knot of spectators around the acrobats resembles a flower, gaining or losing petals as watchers arrive and leave. Its center, where the performers bounce and tumble, is both a pestel and the flower's pistil whose pollen (perhaps the dust they stir up) goes nowhere, but refertilizes its own blossom, leading to a false fruition. This is one of many images comparing and contrasting human life to flowers, trees, fruit, and pollination.

Subrisio Saltat.: an abbreviation of *subrisio saltatoris*, acrobat's smile.

Angel: suppose there's a place: like the Fourth Elegy, the Fifth begins with a vision of unsatisfactory art (in both cases, performance) and closes with a vision in which the difficulties are resolved in the presence of death and a satisfactory performance is envisioned.

Sixth Elegy

To the possible forms of idealized humanity—those who died young, lovers, children, performing artists—whose attempts to fulfill the ideal cause various forms of anguish, Rilke now adds the hero. It is as if the epic hero has suddenly come into the poem, almost as an afterthought. It is a wonderfully subtle portrait, focusing as it does not so much on the hero as on analogies (e.g. the fig tree) and effects (on children, mothers, lovers, and "each heart"). There is something faintly comic about the hero's first asserting himself as a sperm cell. Heroes may be wonderful, but the role is reserved for the few and is as distant, somehow, as a legend.

Karnak: ancient Egyptian holy place, site of many temples and ruins. Rilke had visited it in 1911. The image here seems to be that characteristic depiction of the conqueror, smiling in his chariot as he is pulled by horses who smile the same smile. The smile is another recurrent image in the *Elegies*.

Seventh Elegy

The poem now turns from life-transcendence, as envisioned in the ideal performances and the hero, to life-acceptance. The wooing voice, motivated by desire for a less transient state of being, is rejected, and the poem performs a kind of backward somersault into a beautiful image of a summer dawn. Now the dead seem to long for and seek out our earthly existence. And we are the ones who learn how to love and celebrate the visible, "to transform it within." Human imaginative achievement, as represented by music, architecture, and love, can now be understood and praised.

In the letter to his Polish translator (cited in the Introduction) Rilke wrote:

> Nature, the things we move among and use, are provisional and perishable; but, so long as we are here, they are *our* possession and our friendship, sharing the knowledge of our grief and gladness, as they have already been the confidants of our forebears. Hence it is important not only not to run down and degrade everything earthly, but just because of its temporariness, which it shares with us, we ought to grasp and transform these phenomena and these things in a most loving understanding. Transform? Yes; for our task is so deeply and so passionately to impress upon ourselves this provisional and perishable earth, that its essential being will arise again 'invisibly' in us. *We are the bees of the invisible. We frantically plunder the visible of its honey, to accumulate it in the great golden hive of the invisible.*

Eighth Elegy

The celebration of human transience in the preceding Elegy is here sharply qualified. Self-consciousness, time-consciousness, and death-consciousness, which mark us off from animals and, at times, children and lovers, are Rilke's version of a fallen condition. As he pursues the idea he discovers that even animals may not be altogether at home in this existence because they may have some awareness of the contrast between the comfort of the womb and the exposure of birth. Only creatures like gnats, who come into being in the open air, can be completely at home in the world, taking it for a womb, a mother. If there is a humorous touch in the image of the gnat hopping happily on its wedding day, there is nothing of the kind in the poem's somber and splendid conclusion, one of those summaries of our life that give this poem its impressive scope. This Elegy is dedicated to Rudolf Kassner, an Austrian writer and thinker, because of discussions he and Rilke had at Duino about the preferability of certain states of existence (they did not agree) and such questions as the "happiness of the gnat."

Ninth Elegy

The poem now swings back to something more like the mood of the Seventh Elegy. But praise and pain are tightly woven together by this point in the *Elegies*. We would choose human existence, the opening lines affirm, if we had the alternative of metamorphosis (like Daphne, evading love to become a laurel), but the justification of our choice would not be easy to explain. It becomes clear as the poem moves forward that given our limitation we must accept and celebrate not only our own perishability but that of the things around us. If music, architecture, sculpture, heroism, and love stood for the achievements of the human imagination before, poetry now begins to come into its own as Rilke considers the function of language itself as a means of identification and praise. The letter (quoted in the note, the *Seventh Elegy*) in which Rilke speaks of "the things we move among and use" as "*our* possession and our friendship," is relevant here as well.

Tenth Elegy

Rilke takes several risks in this final Elegy. If the Third Elegy paralleled the epic descent to the underworld, this one seems to take us beyond life and into death in a way that no other poet has attempted. The narrative line and allegorical manner make this Elegy somewhat more accessible, but there is no slackening of imaginative intensity. After an opening 'prayer' of great beauty, we get the wry portrait of "Pain City," and then, in a kind of pastoral 'straying' into strange countryside, we cross that land—based partly on ancient Egypt, the most death-oriented civilization we have had—where visible and invisible are so astonishingly mingled. Motifs from the rest of the poem stream together in this Elegy, as in the list of constellations. And Rilke stretches our imaginative capabilities to their limits, as when we are asked to comprehend that the owl, startled from behind the edge of the Sphinx's crown, traces the shape of the huge face with one wing as it flies across and down it, a tracing which is transferred to the dead man's sharpened sense of hearing as if a book which already lay open could somehow be opened again! The ending of the poem either needs no explanation or simply lies beyond it.